Old St ANDREWS

by

Helen Cook

Evacuees leaving St Andrews railway station on their arrival in the town during the early months of the 1939–45 wa[r]
Station Road, and the children are wearing their evacuee labels and carrying their gas masks, which were issued in [
war broke out. At this time there was an area of pasture opposite the railway station often grazed by sheep where tod
the hostilities there were many air raid alerts in St Andrews and the town suffered bomb damage and some loss of li[fe]

D1219607

© Helen Cook 2001
First published in the United Kingdom, 2001,
by Stenlake Publishing
Telephone / Fax: 01290 551122

ISBN 1 84033 169 0

During periods of keen and sustained frost as in the winter of 1947, this ground adjoining the green of the St Andrews Bowling Club was flooded for skating. There was sledging too at the North Haugh beside Jacob's Ladder until St Andrews University began to develop this area as a science precinct in the mid-1960s. The skaters in the photograph are pupils of St Leonard's School, an independent school for boarding and day pupils founded in 1877. There was also a skating pond on the Lade Braes between the New Mill and the Law Mill, which subsequently became the site of a now vanished rifle practice range.

FURTHER READING

The books listed below were used by the author during her research. None of them are available from Stenlake Publishing. Those interested in finding out more are advised to contact their local bookshop or reference library.

Three Decades of Historical Notes, Ronald G. Cant et al., compiled by Mary M. Innes & Joan A. Whelan, St Andrews Preservation Trust, 1991.
Handbook to the City and University of St Andrews, James Maitland Anderson, 1911.
St John's House, Its History and Archaeology, N. P. Brooks, 1976.
St Leonard's Chapel, St Andrews, R. G. Cant, 1955.
David Hay Fleming, guidebooks to St Andrews, various editions.
Willie Patrick – St Andrews photographer, Matthew Jarron.
St Andrews Preservation Trust Annual Report and Year Book, 1999.
St Andrews Citizen, 1870–
Statistical Account of Scotland, 1793
New Statistical Account of Scotland, 1838.

Articles by the author published in *The Scots Magazine*, *The Courier*, *Country Life*, *St Andrews Citizen* and other newspapers and periodicals, along with personal recollection, have also played their part in the writing of the text of this book.

ACKNOWLEDGEMENTS

The author wishes to thank the St Andrews Preservation Trust for facilities, and its museum curators past and present – Matthew Jarron and Susan Keracher – also the Department of Special Collections and Rare Books of St Andrews University for research facilities. Thanks also to Miss M. Grubb, Mrs B. Willsher, and for family information Mr Gordon Christie, Mrs E. Terris, and Miss Pat Harvey.

The publishers would like to thank the St Andrews Preservation Trust for allowing the use of images from their collection in this book, and Robert Grieves for providing extra information.

INTRODUCTION

The Royal Burgh of St Andrews is a fascinating blend of old and new. 'St Andrews by the northern sea' was an early centre of Christianity in the days of the Celtic Church. A great historic city, whose medieval street plan still exists, it is literally 'the burgh of St Andrew', the patron saint of Scotland. The name St Andrews appears to have been first used to describe the burgh established in the 1130s or 1140s by Bishop Robert to the west of ancient Kinrimund or Kilrymont, where the Church of St Andrew stood.

The town's fortunes have ebbed and flowed over the centuries, but no fingernail sketch of its history would be complete without mention of three landmarks, all of which are now ruined: its great cathedral, St Andrews Castle (the fortified palace of the bishops and archbishops of St Andrews), and St Andrews Priory.

Founded in 1160, the Cathedral Church of St Andrew was consecrated in 1318 in the presence of King Robert the Bruce. The 'new kyrk cathedralle' was the largest in Scotland, and was both the cathedral church of the diocese of St Andrews, and the church of the Priory of Canons Regular of the Order of St Augustine, who served it and formed its chapter. It possessed magnificently enshrined relics of St Andrew and 31 altars, and in medieval times was a centre of pilgrimage and the impressive focal point of the burgh.

1410–14 saw the University of St Andrews, the oldest in Scotland, founded by Bishop Wardlaw, and in 1472 the Bishop of St Andrews was raised to the status of Archbishop and Primate of Scotland. The town became the recognised ecclesiastical capital of Scotland, and until the Reformation St Andrews remained a prosperous, cosmopolitan Scottish burgh with many European connections, a busy harbour, and considerable economic and political importance.

A town well-known to the Scottish kings and queens, here Bishop Wardlaw in his episcopal palace tutored and advised James I, and Bishop Kennedy advised James II how to break the power of the Scottish nobles. Mary, Queen of Scots, whose mother Mary of Lorraine had married James V in St Andrews Cathedral in 1538, holidayed here.

After the Reformation, during the days of episcopacy and Covenanting, stormy and less prosperous times lay ahead for St Andrews. By 1645 its castle was in a bad state of repair, the abandoned cathedral continued to decay, and in 1697/98 there seemed a real possibility that it would lose its university to Perth.

In the eighteenth century St Andrews was in decline for reasons both local and national, and its university experienced difficulties. However during the same period repairs funded by an official national collection were carried out to St Andrews pier and harbour, and it was noted that the town had links 'well known to golfers'.

In c.1821 Dr Lee described St Andrews as: 'A truly academic city, a dark, sombre, ruinous, ill-lighted, badly paved, old fashioned, old mannered, secluded place'. But the wind of change began to blow softly through the quiet old city from the 1830s onwards, and by the end of the century it had emerged as a centre for education, the 'Home of Golf', a popular seaside holiday destination, and a desirable residential town. Even in the last years of the eighteenth century, it was noted that building new houses in St Andrews was profitable. But it was the nineteenth century which saw St Andrews expand beyond its medieval burgh plan, and fine classical terraces and streets of new houses and town mansions began to contrast with the 'quaint roofs . . . and spires' of an older St Andrews. Some of the buildings of United College were rebuilt in 1829–31 and 1845–46, and St Mary's College was repaired and remodelled. Much of this new St Andrews was built of sandstone from the local (but no longer worked) quarries of Nydie and Knockhill, which provided a creamy, warm-toned sandstone which weathers to grey. It was a period when few local builders or stonemasons lacked work. During this century quiet old Georgian St Andrews was cajoled and pushed into the new Victorian age, and there was much burgh housekeeping to be done, as in most towns of the period. A lot was achieved when the great 'improver' of St Andrews Sir Hugh Lyon Playfair was provost (1842–61): slaughtering within the town was forbidden and a new slaughterhouse was provided, a town scavenging service was started, and a better water supply was organised (the water assessment was raised from one old penny to fourpence). 1832, 1842 and 1849 had seen outbreaks of cholera in St Andrews. Throughout the Victorian age the town's public health and amenities continued to be improved.

The nineteenth century saw the building of new schools, churches and hotels, and the establishment of many shops, banks and businesses, a fair number of which would be still trading in the twentieth century, and in some cases the twenty-first century. There was a holiday season and a demand for holiday accommodation.

In 1881 Professor Meiklejohn wrote of St Andrews: 'two great interests share the life of the place – the University and Golf'. The latter grew in popularity in the nineteenth century, nowhere more so than on the St Andrews links. 1873 saw the Open Golf Championship first come to the town, and by the end of the century two new golf courses, in addition to the Old Course, had been laid out at St Andrews, which had become the accepted 'Home of Golf'.

During the nineteenth century the then small university enriched the life of the town through contacts with a wider world outside St Andrews, as it does today. The earlier 1840s saw St Andrews distinguished by the presence of a group of early experimental photographers, who practised calotyping, the photographic process developed by William Henry Fox Talbot of Lacock Abbey. The St Andrews photographers had a link to Talbot through Sir David Brewster, the physicist principal of the university's United College, who was both a friend of Talbot, and a keen photographer himself.

It is interesting to note one or two aspects of an older St Andrews. As one of the oldest seaports in Scotland, the town had a Sea-Box Society from 1643 till 1921, which looked after the welfare of its seagoing members, and from c.1801 to 1938 a succession of lifeboats. Many members of the crews of the latter came from local fisher families. An iron mission church was maintained by the Episcopal Church for both the St Andrews fishing community and the seamen of the trading vessels which then used the harbour.

St Andrews increased in size during the first half of the twentieth century, but between the 1960s and 2001 has rivalled its Victorian expansion in the building of houses and schools, while the university has also increased in size. Never an industrial town, university and other education, golf, and the tourist and conference industry are the staples of the economy of modern St Andrews, with its historic ruins and buildings in the beautiful setting of St Andrews Bay, with the Angus hills to the north.

The Original Coffee Shop opened at 64 Market Street in the mid-1940s. Here red-gowned St Andrews University students are enjoying its amenities. A popular meeting-place, it served coffees, teas, soft drinks, and home baking. The Byre referred to above the counter was, of course, the original Byre Theatre of 1933–69 (see page 44).

Part of the south side of Market Street as it once was between the 'narrow end of Market Street' and Church Street. The old building in the photograph, which stood opposite the 'Double Decker' (see page 7) and was possibly its sibling in age, was demolished in the 1950s to make way for the new premises of a well-remembered St Andrews business, Balone Dairy. This was situated at 56–58 Market Street and was supplied by its own farm. The dairy sold and delivered daily, milk, cream, butter, eggs and morning rolls. The shop also stocked a variety of groceries, including the first frozen foods of the period. On the frontage of the old building the word 'Merchant' can just be made out; here Mr Di Folco had his small grocery before moving to a much larger shop at 104 South Street.

This photograph recalls two well-known St Andrews family businesses, both of which traded in Market Street. The Fairfield Stores had several branches, and was established in Cupar in 1879. At the time of this photograph there was a large drapery hall with a wide range of goods and materials, a men's shop, and a ladies' boutique. The latter occupied the ground floor of the pantiled, crow-stepped building in the photograph with its gable end to the street in the old style. The Fairfield Stores closed in January 1992. Much social change had taken place since Mrs Thomson, proprietrix of the Fairfield Stores, had established her Servants' Registry, which was still in existence in 1939. Alexander the Butcher, whose neighbour was The Original Coffee Shop, traded in Market Street from 1926–87.

Buildings on the north side of Market Street between College Street and Union Street. The picture includes the old building known as the 'Double Decker' because of its distinctive double attics, reminiscent of Continental roofscapes. Union Lane ran behind the west side of Union Street from North Street to Market Street past the Double Decker. It still exists but is no longer a public lane. In the Double Decker's latter days there were three occupied properties in this dark, narrow lane. The distinctive double-roofed building suffered a fire in 1926 and was demolished in conjunction with the slum clearances of the west side of Union Street round about the mid-1930s. One of the shops in this vicinity was Mr and Mrs Barrie's small home bakery; Mr Barrie is remembered for his excellent sultana cake and sponges. Today the university's Buchanan Arts Building, completed in 1964, occupies the site of the Double Decker and the west side of Union Street. It was at the Double Decker that Joan, the fishwife (see page 29) had her fish shop.

Neither the occasion nor the photographer of this event in Market Street are known, but the picture is thought to date from some time during the years 1914–18. The event it records may have been held to raise funds for comforts for soldiers fighting in the First World War. St Andrews' centuries-old town house or tolbooth once stood here. It was a familiar landmark to St Andreans until it was demolished in 1862 on the completion of the present town hall in South Street, which was formally opened on 4 July 1861. Today the outline of the old town house is indicated by coloured cobbles in the roadway. The trees in Market Street were planted in 1897 and removed in 1936.

The west end of Market Street photographed in the late 1940s. This area was once home to a plethora of both privately-owned grocers and branches of national multiples, each with their own individual character. These included three dairy shops, the Maypole, the Buttercup and the 'Danish' shop. All of them specialised in butters, margarines, cream (fresh and tinned) and cheese. Gleaming tiles supplied a fresh dairy-like atmosphere. The former Buttercup premises have become part of the John Smith bookshop, and today the original mosaic doorstep with its logo BDC – Buttercup Dairy Company – still serves as the entrance to the shop. Among the privately-owned grocery stores were C. B. MacFarlane, which latterly incorporated Miss Leslie's Home Bakery; Mr Currie's; and Andrew MacDougall's, which became an early self-service grocery on Mr MacDougall's retirement. Until early in the Second World War Mr McDonald served from his small shop close to Lipton's wearing a crisp white overall. Many other businesses traded in the street, among them coal merchants Rutherford & Grubb, whose window housed fine model railway coal trucks.

This photograph shows two well-known and long-established Market Street businesses, neither of which are still in existence. Charles Robertson's shop served St Andrews for more than one generation, and Johnston's Livery Stables were founded by William Johnston, a blacksmith to trade and an expert four-in-hand driver. The stables were one of the largest such businesses in east Fife. Although essentially a horseman, Johnston recognised the coming importance of the motor vehicle, and by the time of his death in 1917 had acquired several cars for his business. Mr Johnson also farmed Balmungo, and his brother John was riding-master at St Leonard's School.

Johnston's roofed yard was entered from Market Street and the horses reached their stables by way of the slatted ramp. There were harness rooms on the same level as the stalls. The firm subsequently opened a motor garage at 104–108 North Street, with the result that their business premises ran from Market Street through to North Street. Johnston's horse-drawn cabs plied in and around St Andrews until the early years of the 1939–45 war, when the firm ceased to keep cab or riding horses because of the difficulty of feeding them during wartime. Subsequently Johnston's hired taxis, cars and buses, sold and repaired cars, and offered full garage facilities. Today this part of Market Street has been redeveloped.

South Street photographed from near the West Port at a time when lamplighters still climbed their ladders as darkness fell to light the town's gas street lamps. The lime trees give the street a Continental air. The planting of the first of these was advocated and pioneered by the architect and town councillor John Milne (1823–1904) who persuaded South Street property owners to plant limes on the north side of the street in 1879; planting of the south side followed in 1880. The historian, antiquary and writer Dr David Hay Fleming planted his trees with his own hands. In 1914 there were only five electric street lamps in St Andrews and most shops and houses were lit by gas. Three years previously gas had cost four shillings and twopence per 1,000 cubic feet, with a reduction of tenpence if bills were paid within one month to the St Andrews Gas Co. Ltd. The vehicle in the photograph bears an early Fife registration number.

Taken in 1946, this delightful photograph shows Mrs Bennet in her home in Imrie's Close, South Street. Once a barn, the small pantiled house with its crow-stepped gables was the first Secession (Burgher) Kirk in St Andrews from 1749–74. Mrs Bennet is sitting by a small Victorian range, complete with an oven on one side of the fire, and on the other side a tank for heating water. Filled from the top, the water could then be run off from a tap when heated. Such ranges, gleaming with black lead and metal polish and containing a bright fire, were a cheerful focal point in a room but were very labour intensive. Their cooking facilities were often supplemented by a gas ring. The St Andrews Preservation Trust renovated the small house, which is numbered 136 South Street, in 1954.

Blackfriars Chapel in South Street photographed from the grounds of Madras College as it once was – clad with ivy and enclosed by railings. This vaulted apsidal chapel of 1525 was added to the church of the St Andrews house of the Dominicans or Blackfriars, and is the only surviving part of the church, which suffered considerable damage during the Scottish Reformation. Blackfriars Chapel is one of the old 'lions' of St Andrews, and is the subject of an engraving in Francis Grose's *Antiquities of Scotland*, published between 1789–91. The same engraving also depicts the old St Andrews Grammar School, which stood immediately east of the chapel. The school's outhouses (including a roofed stable!) are shown abutting upon and within the chapel. Mystery still surrounds the burial place of Cardinal David Beaton, who was murdered in St Andrews Castle in May 1546. Possibly he was buried quietly in the choir of the church of the Blackfriars, after lying 'unburyit sevin monethis and more' wrapped in lead in the castle's Bottle Dungeon.

A photograph thought to have been taken by Dr John Adamson, captioned 'First Prizers, Madras College' and dated 1858. Madras College was founded in 1832 by the St Andrews-born educational reformer, Revd Dr Andrew Bell (1753–1832). It incorporated the town's Grammar School and English School and was built in the Blackfriars Yards – the grounds and gardens which once belonged to the St Andrews house of the Blackfriars or Dominicans. The school's quadrangle ('The Quad'), part of which can be seen here, gave rise to the old traditional school walk in which girls walked anticlockwise round it and boys clockwise. During the Second World War the quad's arches were bricked up to provide shelter for staff and pupils during air-raids. The college originally used Bell's Madras or monitorial system of teaching – where older pupils taught younger ones – the basis of which Bell had seen in India and then developed. A considerable number of pupils came from outwith St Andrews, some from as far afield as India.

The interior of Holy Trinity Church – the 'Town Kirk' – photographed before its great 1907–09 restoration, carried out during the ministry (1899–1924) of the Revd Dr Patrick Macdonald Playfair, of whom it was said 'his congregation was Patrick Playfair's central sphere'. The restoration returned this important Scottish parish church, founded in 1410–12 by Bishop Wardlaw, as far as possible to its original medieval form after the church's major alterations of 1798–1800. The architect of the twentieth century restoration was P. Macgregor Chalmers, and the restored kirk was rededicated on St Andrew's Day 1909.

The historic St Leonard's Chapel is situated off The Pends. This picture shows it prior to 1910, when it was re-roofed and re-glazed. It is very much part of the history of St Andrews, and served both as the Parish Church of St Leonard (first mentioned in 1413) and the chapel of St Leonard's College. The latter, initially called 'the College of Poor Clerks of the Kirk of St Andrew', was founded as part of St Andrews University in 1512 by Archbishop Alexander Stewart and Prior John Hepburn. Before this, in the age of pilgrimage, the building had been the chapel of the old pilgrim hospice, the Hospital of St Andrew. This later became an almshouse for aged women. After the uniting of St Salvator's and St Leonard's Colleges in 1747 the chapel was abandoned and stood roofless from c.1762 until its restoration in 1910. The university undertook further renovation in 1948, and on 6 November 1952 – St Leonard's Day – the chapel and its memorial furnishings were rededicated.

The funeral of 'Old Tom' Morris (1821–1908) on its way to the cathedral burying ground, passing Holy Trinity Church during its 1907–09 rebuilding. The cortège is also passing the *St Andrews Citizen* building (visible more clearly on page 17) before its 1928 redesign. This building stands on the site of the house owned and occupied in the eighteenth century by barber Baillie Bell, whose second son Dr Andrew Bell founded Madras College. The Bell home was described as having 'an outer staircase supported by wooden pillars and a wooden projection into the street'. Printing and publishing have long been connected with this location. As well as barbering, Baillie Bell mended watches and assisted another St Andrean, Alexander Wilson, in his attempts to perfect his scheme for casting types. As a result of his work, Wilson earned the description 'the father of Scottish letter founders'. At an earlier date (1620) Edward Raban of Edinburgh, 'printer to the university', set up his printing press on the same site. The *St Andrews Citizen* was founded in 1870 by John Innes of J. & G. Innes, printers, publishers, stationers and booksellers.

The annual St Andrews Lammas Market is the oldest Scottish medieval town market in existence, and is now an amalgam of fairground amusements and stalls selling goods. 'Market Day', the last day of the four-day fair, is always the second Tuesday in August. Visiting the market is a tradition for many St Andreans, and memories of past occasions include the magnificent black traction engine which once powered the 'jungle ride' in Market Street, and the fair people's caravans which were parked in North Street. Fascinating glimpses were caught of neat interiors, gleaming with mirrors and glass, and burnished range-like stoves which burnt coal. Bright pink sugar hearts, 'Market' sweeties, and gingerbreads, sold both by local shops and fair stalls, were once all part of the fun of the fair. Pitches for the market were auctioned in a public roup at so much per linear foot and were measured out for each stall-holder or amusement-owner

under the supervision of the burgh surveyor. Attendance at the annual auctioning of the South Street stances early on Monday morning was a traditional ritual for many St Andreans. Mr James Macgregor of John Macgregor of 71 Market Street (later 71–73 Market Street), cabinetmakers, upholsterers, undertakers, auctioneers, valuators and house factors, the gentleman with the moustache second from the right in the picture, long conducted the auction of the stances with wit and good humour. Jim Walsh, assistant auctioneer, is the man in the light coloured suit, while the third person is well-known St Andrews personality Bailie David Fraser, who had a great interest in the Lammas Market. The policeman on the extreme left is PC Adamson. Many walked on the Sunday before Market Day to view and count the fair caravans and vans waiting in line outside the town, ready to enter it on Monday morning to bid for a South Street stance. This Lammas Market photograph was taken before 1938.

16

True gypsies telling fortunes have long been part of the St Andrews Lammas Market. From *c.*1836–37 until *c.*1916 the event was a feeing market and fair in the style of the now long gone St James's Market in Cupar, and country people came in to the Lammas to find new jobs and employers. By the early 1930s the decorated carts of country people coming into town for the fair were seldom seen. In the later 1890s part of the *St Andrews Citizen* building was used as a printing office, thus renewing a tradition of printing on the site going back to the seventeenth century. Today the redesigned shop selling books, newspapers, stationery and gifts, with its carved exterior figure of St Andrew, is a landmark on the corner of South Street and Church Street.

St Andrews University celebrated the quincentenary of its founding (1410–1414) over four days in September 1911. This photograph of St Mary's College and the former university library was first published in the *Handbook to the City and University of St Andrews*, written by university librarian James Maitland Anderson for the benefit of the quincentenary guests. Twenty-seven photographs illustrated the handbook, 23 of which were specially commissioned from Willie Patrick, who was described by the book's author as 'a local amateur [photographer] of exceptional skill'. Until 1976, when it moved to North Street, the university library was sited east of St Mary's College. This picture provides a good view of its then new 1907–09 Carnegie extension, designed by Sir Robert Lorimer. The extension suffered some damage in an air raid in 1940.

Hogmanay used to be much more of a children's festival than it is today. In St Andrews, children would rise early on Hogmanay – Cake Day – to make a round of the shops reciting:

> Ma feet's cauld, ma shune's thin,
> Gie's ma cakes and let me rin!

The 'cakes' were often a penny, an orange, or one of the special biscuits and buns made by the St Andrews bakers for the occasion. This 1936 photograph shows children receiving their cakes from the grocer's shop of William Birrell at 89 South Street, one of many such shops which served the town before the coming of the supermarkets. The years after the 1939–45 war saw the gradual disappearance of Cake Day, an old custom of a smaller and quieter St Andrews, although in the 1950s a small number of children in the town and the East Neuk of Fife still kept the tradition. There were many variations of the Cake Day rhyme, one of which had eleven lines.

Left: Baker Lane in the heart of old St Andrews, photographed before extensive redevelopment by the town council in the mid-1950s, during which many of the lane's old houses were demolished. The building on the east side with the street lamp was the old model lodging house, which stood at the corner of Baker Lane and the narrow end of Market Street. It has been replaced by modern flats. Today the lane is an attractive mix of houses of different periods, enhanced with spring flowering cherry trees and open garden ground on the west side where demolished houses were not replaced by new ones. Baxter is Scots for baker, and over the centuries Baker Lane has been known as Baxter Wynd, Bakehouse Wynd and Bakers Wynd.

This now much altered South Street frontage was once home to two well-known St Andrews shops. T. T. Fordyce was provost of St Andrews from 1961–70 and the Fordyces, 'Family, School, and University Outfitters and General Drapers', had one shop in Cupar and two in St Andrews. This branch was situated at 65 South Street and the Drapery House was located at no. 135. Nos. 67–69 South Street were acquired by the university in 1970. Thought to date from the eighteenth or nineteenth century, renovation and reconstruction revealed a stone building possibly originating from the fifteenth century. The restored property incorporating the former shops is now known as St John's House, signifying that at one period in its history it had belonged to the Order of Knights of the Hospital of St John in Jerusalem, whose symbol was the Maltese cross. The fifteenth-century owner of the house was both a wealthy draper and a provost of St Andrews.

The St Andrews photographer Willie Patrick (1869–1953) took this charming photograph of a group of unknown bathing belles on the West Sands in the summer of 1909. Did they make use of the bathing machines shown below? These were succeeded by equally old fashioned green and white striped versions with steps, and damp, sandy interiors, which were in use on the West Sands until the outbreak of the 1939–45 war. As the tide rose and fell the machines were pulled up and down to the sea by a patient horse for the convenience of bathers.

A tranquil view of St Andrews photographed from the West Sands, the bathing machines suggestive of summer pleasures. In 1838 the lack of the 'very appropriate conveniences' of such machines at St Andrews was remarked upon. The tower and spire of St Salvator's College punctuates the skyline, and the Royal and Ancient Clubhouse (built 1854, with later additions), is visible to the right. To the left of St Salvator's tower stands the white gable end of the temporary Roman Catholic chapel erected by the 3rd Marquis of Bute in 1884–85. This was built on the site of a former roller skating rink, erected in 1876 by a company from Middlesborough. The skates used were Plymton's Patent, and the rink's floor was of smooth pitch pine instead of the usual asphalt. Tennis was also played in the building.

Mrs LEO BLISS'S 'BUSY BEES' ST ANDREWS, 1927.

A 1927 photograph of the pierrot company Mrs Leo Bliss's 'Busy Bees', performing in the then new Beach Pavilion close to the Step Rock. In the 1930s the pierrots presented afternoon and evening programmes in the pavilion, although their fortunes waxed and waned in tandem with those of the Step Rock Pool. By the 1950s a summer season of variety was being presented in the town hall, and the Beach Pavilion, with its inadequate facilities and unroofed seating, had been abandoned. Only a memory too is the once popular walk for locals and visitors down by the Step Rock, with a stop to watch the pierrots as a standing audience outside the terracing fence of the Beach Pavilion – an audience who were expected to drop a copper or two into the pierrots' collecting boxes!

Donkeys patiently wait for young riders on the West Sands. Until recently donkey-rides were as much a part of a seaside summer holiday as ice cream cones and sliders, bathing and paddling, building sandcastles and watching the pierrots. On the Monday and Tuesday of the August Lammas Market the donkeys left the sands for the Victorian Queen's Gardens in the town. There children could enjoy rides on them, and maybe have their photograph taken on their donkey by an itinerant photographer. It was all part of the fun of the fair. Then as now the fair was held in Market and South Street. The seaside donkeys were present in Queen's Gardens for the Lammas Market as recently as 1977.

In the summers of yesterday a very popular late July/early August sporting event took place on the West Sands. This was competitive motorcycle racing, and motorcyclists homed in from all the airts to compete in the Saturday afternoon event, which took place on a great expanse of smooth sand left by an ebbing tide. Thousands of spectators poured into St Andrews by road and rail to watch the motorcyclists competing in the Scottish Motor Cycle Speed Championship events, and the splutter and roar of the machines could even be heard in town. It was an event which had a history dating back to 1909, when the enterprising Christie brothers, James and Jack, 'Motor and Cycle Agents', were given permission by the town council to hold motorcycle races on the West Sands organised by Leven Motor Cycle Club. James and Jack were builders of handmade 'Bell Rock Cycles', and were early motorcycle enthusiasts. No racing took place during the Second World War, but afterwards organised motorcycle racing survived in some form or another into the 1950s.

Motor racing on the West Sands is an event that has long ceased but is not forgotten. 29 July 1950 saw crowds watching the annual motor race along the sands. The 30-mile event was sponsored by the Lothian Car Club, and the film star Jean Kent presented the winner, from Duns, with his trophy. His average speed had been 60 m.p.h.

When the sun shone in summers past the Step Rock – with its swimming and paddling pools and changing facilities – was a Mecca for St Andreans and holidaymakers alike. The sea-water swimming pool enjoyed its heyday in the 1930s and 40s. It was more than seven feet deep at one end, and the daily temperatures of the water were chalked up on a slate near the changing rooms. Deck chairs could be hired, and 'shivery-bites', ice-cream and lemonade, trays of tea and coffee, biscuits and sweets, could be bought from the kiosk. Swimming galas, water polo, life-saving and diving displays, inter-swimming club events and the occasional bathing belle competition were all part of the Step Rock's attractions. However, as holiday tastes and expectations changed from the 1950s onwards, the pool declined in popularity and has since been superseded by the new indoor pool at the East Sands Leisure Centre.

Right: An atmospheric photograph of now-disappeared fisher houses in North Street and their occupants. The little girls would not have had far to go to school – just along the road by way of the Leddyheid (Ladyhead) to the East Infant or East End School in Gregory Place. This developed from the Fisher School – 'the school laid down for the fishers themselves' – in the 1840s. At the time attendance at school was voluntary and not entirely free of charge, with the result that most fisher children had desultory schooling. The Fisher School, which was also used for evening classes, still stands, although the East Infant School has made way for housing. The buildings in this photograph have been replaced by the University's Younger Hall of 1929, its later Gannochy Building, and the rectory of All Saints Episcopal Church.

Another view of the old North Street fishing quarter, the Ladyhead, part of the Fishergate. The old Fish Cross, which was removed *c.*1800, once stood somewhere in the foreground. Fish caught by St Andrews fishermen would have been bought and sold around the cross. The picture looks east along North Street to the spires of St Andrews Cathedral and the 'Square Tower' of St Rule or St Regulus. Much has changed in this eastern section of North Street, which intersects with North and South Castle Street (also part of the old fishing quarter). No longer is the name Gregory Green in common use for the once partially grassed wide eastern extremity of North Street. Gone too are the tiny old fisher cottages adjacent to the cart. Today, however, a number of former fisher houses in the old Fishergate have been beautifully restored, including the St Andrews Preservation Trust Museum at 12 North Street.

Mending nets and baiting lines were everyday tasks for St Andrews fisher families. Note the heap of mussels and the strings of split haddocks hung up to dry in this North Street photograph. The curing of haddock on a larger scale began in the town in the summer of 1888, when William Glen, a fish curer from Eyemouth (famous for its lightly smoked haddock – Eyemouth Pales) took over the tenancy of the Shore Mill at St Andrews harbour, employing a number of fisher women and girls. In 1937 when old fisher houses in this part and side of North Street were being demolished, recognisable stones from the ruins of St Andrews Cathedral were found built into their walls, including pieces of columns and mouldings. For generations after the Reformation the abandoned cathedral was regarded as a convenient stone quarry.

Three St Andreans bringing home the mussels. Originally bait mussels were gathered free from the Eden mussel scalps by the St Andrews fisher people. However from the 1840s onwards, amidst much bitter dissension, the town council issued a spate of regulations and bye-laws to limit and regulate this activity. The mussels ceased to be free, and the council appointed a keeper at the Eden scalps. In 1871 some St Andrews fishermen were imprisoned for ten days for taking mussels without paying for them. They claimed that with an average weekly wage of ten shillings they couldn't afford to pay eight or nine pence per basket of mussels. Selling bait became a good source of revenue for the town, and in 1882 local fishermen bought 2,160 baskets of Eden mussels, and 'strangers' 1,265. Quite apart from use as bait, mussels feature in traditional Scottish shellfish soups, with an old recipe for Mussel Brose combining mussels and oatmeal.

The activity in the foreground of this photograph of fisher women suggests the preparation of fish for sale, as does the creel, basket and barrow. Nineteenth century fishing families in St Andrews included the Melvilles, Browns, Wilsons, Duffs, Gourlays, Hutchinsons, Chisholms, Cunninghams, Kirks, Fentons, Gordons, and Lyalls, among others. To the left of the photograph there is a glimpse of the old East Poorhouse – the 'Home of Rest', where both men and women were cared for within living memory. Some inmates helped with the domestic chores in the home, whose floors and stairs are remembered as being of simple, well scrubbed wood. Today the renovated building is privately-owned housing.

This photograph of a fisherwoman carrying her creel was taken at the back of the 'Royal George' tenement. Fisher women played a vital economic role in helping to sell the fish, and also baited lines. In Victorian times they walked out via the links and West Sands to the Eden estuary mussel scalps where, bare-legged and bare-footed, they gathered bait mussels and carried them home in creels on their backs. It was a round journey of about four miles. From time immemorial, prior to the building of the West Sands Road in the twentieth century, there was a well-trodden way – the Mussel Road – out to the Eden Point. 1884 saw the important International Fisheries Exhibition take place in London, and arrangements were made for six St Andrews fisher women to visit the event.

Willie Patrick delighted in photographing everyday life in old St Andrews, and many of his surviving photographs are of the town's now vanished fishing community (the pictures on pages 25 (right), 27 (right), 30 (left), 31 and 32 (right) were also taken by him). This example shows members of four well-known St Andrews fishing families; Mrs Kirk, Mrs Stevenson, Mrs Fenton, and Mrs Cunningham, and was taken at the back of the 'Royal George' tenement at St Andrews harbour. This had been converted from a former granary in the nineteenth century and contained two-roomed fisher houses with box beds. The houses had no storage for fishing gear, which was left under a wall at the back of the building in dry weather. When it was wet the nets had to be kept inside the cramped houses. It was once quite common for domestic buildings in multiple occupancy to be given nicknames. The Royal George was named after the naval vessel of the same name which capsized with her hundred guns on 29 August 1782 when lying at Spithead undergoing a repair. Almost all her crew were aboard, along with many visiting women and children, and she sank almost immediately with the loss of about 900 lives. It wasn't until 1848 that the wreck was finally raised. In the 1930s many old houses in St Andrews were condemned, including those in the Royal George, which was emptied of its occupants in 1935 but not demolished. During the mid-1960s it was rebuilt as houses and flats along with Mr Bonella's small adjoining mill (which milled all grades of oatmeal from oat flour to pinhead oatmeal), the former coastguard office and store, and The Auld Hoose public house.

Mrs Henry Waters Clark – 'Joan, the fishwife' – died in 1927 aged 75. She was probably the best-known and remembered St Andrews fishwife (and on her death was said to be the last). Mrs Clark liked her name pronounced Jo-ann in the Scottish style, and was known for her spotless cleanliness and neat fisherwife dress. This consisted of short, brightly coloured, bunchy petticoats, red knitted jacket, elastic-sided boots and spotless white stockings. Her colourful outfit

meant that she was often the subject of paintings. Known for her ready wit, Joan was a member of a well-known fishing family and was skilled at baiting lines. She had a fish shop in Market Street for some years, but sold most of her fish from her wheelbarrow, and would deliver to customers. Her home 'Joan's House', 11 South Castle Street, was a one-roomed dwelling as neat as herself. It was one of the first properties to be bought by the St Andrews Preservation Trust, and with its pantiles and outside stair remains a picturesque reminder of the old fishing quarter. By the time of Joan's death fishing at St Andrews was only a shadow of its former self, as summed up by these contemporary local comments: 'nae fish in St Andrews Bay noo', and 'fishing with small yawls has ceased to provide a living wage'. As the fishing declined a number of local fishermen became full- or part-time caddies on the links or took up other occupations; Joan's son Henry was a golf club maker. After Joan's death Arbroath fishwives wearing traditional dress made regular visits to St Andrews to sell fish including Arbroath smokies. One of the best known was a Mrs Swankie.

Dating from the early years of the twentieth century, this picture shows the Royal George tenement overlooking the harbour, along with the two Shorehead public houses. The Bell Rock Tavern stands at the north (far) end of the tenement, with the whitewashed Auld Hoose at its near end. Formerly a granary and storage buildings, the Royal George was converted to fisher houses in the 1860s by George Bruce (1825–1904), builder and prominent long-time member of St Andrews Town Council. He had a great interest in maritime matters and the local fishing community, and was the author of *Reminiscences of St Andrews Bay with the History of the Lifeboat, and a sketch of the Fishing Population in the City.* Ship figureheads adorned the garden of his home in the narrow end of Market Street. To the left of the picture is the now demolished St Andrews Gasworks with its obtrusive chimney. Gas was made here from 1835 to February 1962. The first gasmaker was Will Fowlis, who was paid £50 per annum.

Washing hanging out to dry at the back of the Royal George. The boy is walking past the end of The Auld Hoose pub; the house next to that was used by the coastguard as an office and store. The old Customs House, which was in use when St Andrews had a busy trade with the Continent, was also once part of this harbour block. The building at the top of the slope on the left belonged to the St Andrews Gas Company.

A Willie Patrick photograph taken in the inner harbour c.1909–14 showing Robert Cunningham on the left and H. Gourlay on the right. During the nineteenth century the St Andrews fishing boats gradually increased in size and number, and the local fishing was relatively prosperous. Line fishing was used for haddock, cod, ling, skate, halibut, flounder and plaice, and the bay also yielded lobsters and partans. In addition to local line fishing, St Andrews boats sailed as far afield as Shetland and the English coast for the seasonal herring fishing. In 1881 the newly-built St Andrews boats *Our Queen*, *Sea King* and *Fisher Lassie* were among those that sailed for the herring and haddock fishing. Of considerable size, they were Cellardyke and St Monan's built. At the time *Our Queen* was the largest boat built to order for any Fife fisherman. In 1882 skipper A. Gordon's *Fisher Lassie* landed a total catch of 400 crans of summer herring, while Alex Greig's *Pride of the Ocean* landed 300 crans. The 1897 winter herring fishing was good, and St Andrews boats fished from Anstruther in company with vessels from Newhaven, Buckhaven and Broughty Ferry. St Andrews boats sailing to the herring fishing received a great send-off from the harbour from their families, a time when 'herrin' bakes' (hard-baked biscuits) were showered onto the pier. The twentieth century saw the gradual decline of the local fishing.

David Black, fisherman, photographed in 1917 by Willie Patrick. In the 1870s Mr Black lived at 12 North Street, today the museum of the St Andrews Preservation Trust. At one time the property housed four fisher families. As a member of the St Andrews fishing community, David Black is wearing a reefer jacket and peaked cap.

Left: William Malloch, the first rescue at the Step Rock. Born *c.*1860, William went to sea when he was twelve and was appointed to his post at the Step Rock in 1887, then an undeveloped bathing and swimming place for men and boys. He remained the rescue for sixteen years, and is reputed to have saved 191 lives. St Andrews Swimming Club was instituted in 1856. 1902 saw the construction of the Step Rock Bathing Pool, which in its early days was only for male bathers and swimmers. The depth of the pool graduated from 2 feet 4 inches to 8 feet, and its dimensions were 300 by 100 feet.

The paddle steamer *Carrick Castle* at St Andrews pier. Pleasure trips in such boats used to make popular holiday excursions. The lengthening of the Long Pier at St Andrews had been completed by 1900.

The *Prinses Wilhelmina* of Halmnstad, Sweden, left Kime (Finland) on 12 September 1912 with a cargo of firewood for the Dundee firm Langland & McAinsh. She reached the Tay on a day of storm, which prevented a pilot reaching her to take her upriver to Dundee. Aware of the dangers of a stormy St Andrews Bay for sailing ships, her captain put to sea again in an attempt to reach a safe anchorage in the Firth of Forth, but his attempts were unsuccessful and the *Prinses Wilhelmina* had to ride out the north-easterly gale in the bay instead. On 30 September the 366 ton ship struck the rocks below St Andrews Castle, close to where the *Merlin* had been wrecked in March 1881 with the loss of her crew of eleven. However, the St Andrews lifeboat *John and Sarah Hatfield* (see overleaf) reached her and rescued her crew of nine. Later the wreck floated off the rocks and grounded on the West Sands, where the ship's cat was found alive and well. Much of the barque's cargo was salvaged, and her wreck (which was both photographed and painted) was the source of many souvenirs.

The St Andrews lifeboat the *John and Sarah Hatfield* in the harbour. Over the years she saved 43 lives and helped many vessels in distress, including the *Prinses Wilhelmina*. In 1914 she was called out six times and saved sixteen lives, thirteen from the destroyer HMS *Success*, which was driven ashore at Kingsbarns during a December hurricane. In 1915 she went to the assistance of a seaplane.

Crowds gathered to watch the final practice launch of the last St Andrews lifeboat, the *John and Sarah Hatfield* from the East Sands in the summer of 1938. This was the year that St Andrews ceased to be a lifeboat station, a sad and nostalgic event for the town. At the time of her withdrawal the *John and Sarah Hatfield* had been stationed in the town for 28 years. Her last coxswain was David Fenton, who had been a lifeboat crew member since 1898. After her withdrawal, the lifeboat was sold as a private pleasure craft and her gear auctioned in the town. Her carriage fetched £1. The stone and slate lifeboat house still stands.

ST. ANDREWS. FROM THE EAST. 926. G.W.W.

This tranquil view is from the studio of George Washington Wilson, photographers to Queen Victoria in Scotland. It shows the East Bents and East Sands, which stretch from the Kinkell Braes to St Andrews harbour. St Nicholas Farm and farmhouse can be seen on the left. Three hospitals have been associated with this area. The early twelfth century St Nicholas Hospital was in use until *c.*1580 and provided care for lepers and the sick poor. In 1882 the threat of a typhus outbreak in the town (in the event it didn't occur) saw the building of a temporary wooden hospital on the East Bents, while a more permanent city fever hospital was built in St Mary's Street in 1885. The timber hospital was used by Professor W. C. McIntosh as a pioneer marine laboratory. 1896 saw a specially designed laboratory, the Gatty Marine Laboratory, the gift of Dr C. H. Gatty, built at the East Bents. Dr McIntosh was both a much-loved St Andrews family doctor and a distinguished researcher in marine biology. The growing size and prosperity of Victorian St Andrews saw the well-remembered Woodburn Laundry established at Woodburn, while nearby on the East Bents was the St Andrews lifeboat house. New housing, an extension to the Gatty Marine Laboratory, Albany Park, and the East Sands Leisure Centre are among the recent developments in this area.

Another photograph by Willie Patrick, this time showing Miss Grant Suttie winning the Ladies' Scottish Championship of 1911 at St Andrews by a putt. The runner-up was Miss Ida Kyle, a St Andrews lady from a prominent golfing family. The ladies were very evenly matched, and crowds followed the players in the closing rounds of the championship. While Ida was the runner-up in 1911, Elsie Kyle won the championship in 1909 and 1910, and Audrey Kyle was runner-up in 1922. The male members of the Kyle family were also distinguished in amateur golf. This was one of the photographs which Willie Patrick contributed to the old *Fife News and Coast Chronicle Illustrated Almanacs* published by J. & G. Innes of Cupar.

Are the car's unidentified occupants golfing St Andreans or visitors? The vehicle is a 1904 Argyll which was built in Bridgeton, Glasgow, before the company moved to Alexandria. It is parked in The Links outside the New Golf Club, which was formed in 1902. Golf, 'an elegant amusement and conducive to health', began its widespread growth in popularity in the nineteenth century, a century which saw the forming of what were then called 'artisan' golf clubs in St Andrews. The Thistle Club was instituted in 1817, dissolved in 1839 and reconstituted in 1865, and the St Andrews Golf Club, originally named the Mechanics Club, formed in 1843. All three clubs are still in existence today. In 1834 the Society of St Andrews Golfers (dating from 1754), whose members were 'the noblemen and gentlemen of Fife, and the neighbouring counties', saw William IV agree to become the patron of the society as the Royal and Ancient Golf Club of St Andrews. By the time the New Golf Club had been formed, St Andrews had become the accepted 'Home of Golf'.

A Victorian photograph of the staff of R. Forgan & Son taken outside the company's premises in The Links overlooking the 18th green of the Old Course. In 1819 Hugh Philp was appointed clubmaker to the Society of St Andrews Golfers (later the Royal and Ancient Golf Club). His nephew Robert Forgan (1825–1900) – the white-bearded and hatted gentleman in the second row from the back – trained as a joiner before starting to work for Philp. Robert inherited his uncle's business and expanded it into the celebrated R. Forgan & Sons, manufacturers of golf clubs and balls. Forgan was clubmaker to the Prince of Wales (later Edward VII), and following this appointment in 1863 the Prince's feathers were impressed on Forgan clubheads and also occupied a prominent place on the outside of the Forgan building. Robert Forgan & Son remained a family business until 1962. Today the company name is visible on the pavement outside the former premises.

Right: The singer Bing Crosby with St Andrews stonemason James K. Wilson (usually known as J. K.), one of the town's prominent amateur golfers. The latter entered the 1950 Amateur Golf Championship at St Andrews and his first round draw was against Bing Crosby. J. K. beat Bing 3 and 2, and at the same time sowed the seeds of a lifelong friendship with the star. Wilson played with Crosby on various Scottish golf courses and persuaded him to present a trophy for a new St Andrews competition – the Bing Crosby Seniors Tournament. This photograph was taken in front of the Royal and Ancient Clubhouse on the steps leading down to the Old Course.

A photograph of Old Tom Morris (1821–1908) taken by Willie Patrick not long before Morris's death. He was called 'Old Tom' to distinguish him from his brilliant golf professional son 'Young Tom', who died aged 24 on Christmas Day 1875. Tom Morris returned to his native St Andrews from Prestwick in 1865 when he was appointed keeper of the green of the Old Course and the Royal and Ancient's honorary golf professional. He was skilled in greenkeeping and laying out courses, and as a professional had won the Open Championship in 1861, 1862, 1864 and 1867. Morris also made golf clubs and balls, and set up premises for this purpose overlooking the 18th green of the Old Course. Old Tom's words to his greenkeeping foreman on the subject of keeping the turf in fine condition have become legendary: 'Saund, Honeyman, saund, and then mair saund'. The former Grand Hotel of 1894 (just left of centre) is now Hamilton Hall, a student hall of residence.

The 15th green and 16th fairway of the Old Course photographed before the St Andrews to Leuchars railway line (which had opened in July 1852) closed in 1969. The line divided the Eden Golf Course in two, and a wooden bridge was provided for the use of golfers and walkers. Just discernible to the left of the Royal and Ancient Clubhouse is the small single-storey building that was once The Bay Tea Room. In the 1930s Mrs McBride dispensed tea, scones, cakes, lemonade and ice cream from here. Later it was the first headquarters of the St Andrews Links Trust, and its site is now occupied by the British Golf Museum. The tearoom and adjoining public toilets can be seen more clearly at the right-hand edge of the picture on page 22.

West Park was built as a family home by Major Holcroft, one of a number of army and naval officers who settled in St Andrews from the later eighteenth century onwards. Major Holcroft (then a captain) married Frances (Fanny) Austen, a relative of the novelist Jane Austen, in 1808. Fanny and her marriage is mentioned by Jane in a letter. The Holcrofts left St Andrews in 1837 and 'Major Holcroft's park' (hence West Park) was sold for development. Between 1847 and 1898 Lockhart Place, Hope Street, Abbotsford Crescent and Howard Place were built there. These were 'houses of a superior description', designed to induce families of 'rank and fortune' to settle in St Andrews. Captain Stewart, a later occupant of the Holcroft home, planted lime trees in front of both West Park House and its neighbour the West Infant School. Over the years the house underwent various alterations and renovations, latterly becoming West Park Hotel. It was demolished in 1966 to make way for a new students' union building.

A Victorian photograph of a partially developed Queen's Terrace, taken from the Kinness Burn area. The terrace was built on what was then the southern perimeter of old St Andrews, and much of the ground in the vicinity was worked as market gardens. With Greenside Place, Queen's Terrace was developed along part of the easterly section of the walk running beside the town's mill lade, which had for centuries provided water power for various mills on its long route to the harbour. The Episcopal Church of St Andrew (right) was built between 1867 and 1869 and had a tower added to it in 1892 (see page 48). The sycamore tree outside the church still flourishes, and is noted for its early breaking into leaf. Thomas Hodge the Victorian golf artist and prominent member of the Royal and Ancient Golf Club stayed at Westview, a cul-de-sac off this end of Queen's Terrace, where he established Thomas Hodge's School for Young Gentlemen. This catered specifically for pupils intending to follow a military career. For a time Lade Braes Lane was known as Hodge's Close. Today much of the garden ground in the photograph has been built on.

Members of the St Andrews Bowling Club photographed on their green, possibly for the throwing of the first jack at the opening of the season. The green was laid out in 1887 and influenced the naming of Bowling Green Terrace. Included in the picture are several well-known citizens of the day. Mr Bell (second left) and Mr Currie (eighth from left) were both grocers in Market Street. The author remembers, while her mother had her groceries made up, sitting as a small girl on a chair at Mr Bell's counter eating a small paper twist of chocolate drops provided by the proprietor. David Fraser (fourth from right) was a well-known St Andrews town councillor and Fife county councillor. He was Provost of St Andrews from 1955 to 1958 and a keen supporter of the Lammas Market. The part of Queen's Terrace visible in the background can be seen in the picture opposite at an earlier date; here more houses have been built and one property has acquired a conservatory.

The first Byre Theatre (1933–69) was founded by the late A. B. Paterson and supported by the amateur St Andrews Play Club. It was a converted byre or cowshed which was part of Abbey Street Dairy Farm, a burgh farm that was untenanted at the time. The much loved theatre and the steading in which it stood was demolished when medieval Abbey Street was widened in 1969–70 and a companion scheme of new houses built. A new and larger Byre Theatre (1970–1996) was constructed a short distance north of its predecessor at the same time. This was modelled on the Mermaid Theatre in London and opened by the Scottish actor Andrew Cruickshank. The doocot and a tethering ring from Abbey Street Dairy Farm were incorporated into the new theatre.

The northern section of Abbey Street prior to its 1969 widening, looking towards the junction with South Street. Abbey Street was once within the priory boundary and its earliest name was Priors Wynd. Later it became part of the barony of St Leonard's College. When buildings on the east side of the street (including the Crown Hotel) were being demolished as part of the widening scheme, another section of the wall which enclosed the precinct of the Priory of Canons Regular of the Order of St Augustine, who served St Andrews Cathedral, was revealed. The site of the tall house beside the road signs has been incorporated into the new and third Byre Theatre, opened in Summer 2001, while other buildings on this side of Abbey Street have undergone renovation and redevelopment since the photograph was taken. The junction of the west side of Abbey Street with South Street was long marked by the bakery and shop of John W. Macarthur.

Mr E. P. Harvey, agricultural engineer of Greenside Works with his 'St Andrews Improved Seeder'. Mr Harvey's invention, 'designed and produced with maximum simplicity', was intended for all those who grew root crops. It had seating for its operator, so that seed flow could be kept under supervision. Constructed almost entirely of steel, the seeders were hand made at the Greenside Works, and won Mr Harvey a Fife Agricultural Society Silver Medal in 1950. A 'Standard 4 Row Machine' cost £55, and a 'Special 7 Row Machine' £96. Mr Harvey's invention was developed with the help of Fife farmers, and was tested on local farms.

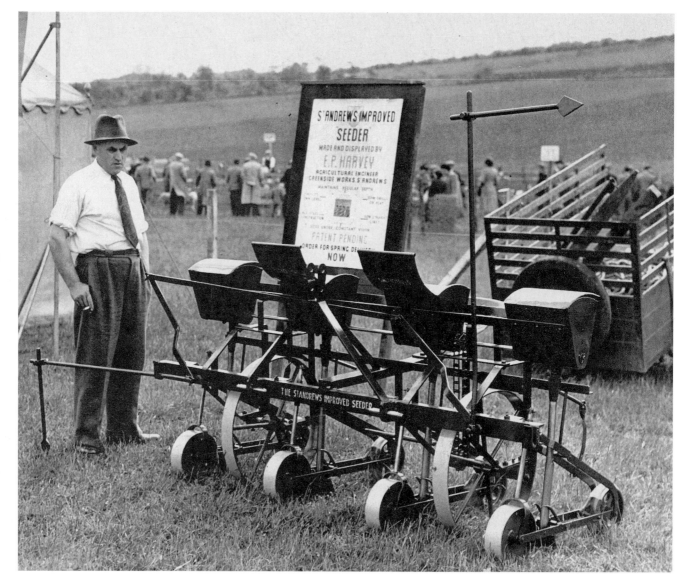

Rachel Nicoll (née Myles) was the wife of the miller at the Law Mill, one of the St Andrews burgh mills. The Nicoll (sometimes spelt Nicol) family occupied the mill with its waterwheel from about the mid-nineteenth century as corn and barley millers. Betsey Nicoll of the Law Mill was a pupil of Madras College, and won a prize for writing in 1859. Thomas Nicoll was recorded as the miller in 1866. The doo-ports above Rachel's head in this *c.*1900 photograph indicate the presence of a doo-laft (pigeon loft) at the mill. These were once commonly found on farm steadings, country buildings and mills. Once on the outskirts of the town, the mill, which ceased working many years ago, lost its rural setting with the development of St Andrews.

Below: Taken from the north side of Argyle Street, this photograph shows Argyle Farm, one of several small burgh farms in St Andrews. Farmer Thomas Ritchie had his house, garden and steading here in the 1920s. In 1959 the cowman's house and the crow-stepped byre were renovated, and there is a row of restored farm cottages on the opposite side of the road. Ritchie's farm was one of three such steadings in Argyle Street, and there were others elsewhere in the town. By the 1950s none of the town farms were still in use. In the winter of 1883 one of two cows belonging to 'Mr W. Ritchie, farmer, Argyle' made local news by her escape on arrival by rail at St Andrews. She was found some days later in nearby countryside.

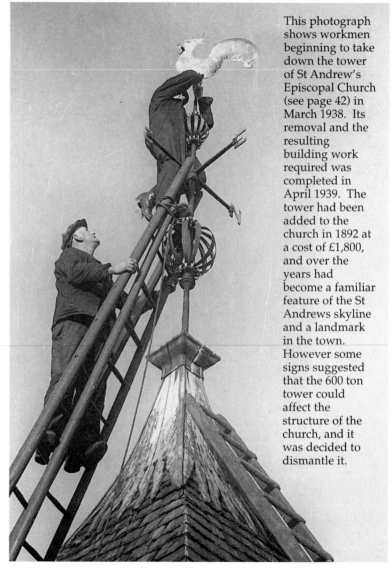

Bell Street showing the now-demolished Congregational Church, which was in use as a church from 1854 until 1966. Its last minister was Miss Helen Woods BD, the first woman to be ordained in St Andrews and only the second in Scotland. Over the years Bell Street has been home to many well-remembered shops, including 'Caird's at Bell Street' which closed in 1984, a sizeable branch of the firm A. Caird & Sons of Dundee. Their January sale was quite a local event at a time when sales didn't take place every other day. At one time payments were placed in metal canisters, which whizzed up a tube to an unseen office to be returned with change and receipt. Bell Street was named after Dr Andrew Bell, founder of Madras College. Until recently Donaldson & Son, 'Shoemakers of Quality', occupied the premises on the corner of this side of Bell Street and South Street. The firm was established in 1841.

This photograph shows workmen beginning to take down the tower of St Andrew's Episcopal Church (see page 42) in March 1938. Its removal and the resulting building work required was completed in April 1939. The tower had been added to the church in 1892 at a cost of £1,800, and over the years had become a familiar feature of the St Andrews skyline and a landmark in the town. However some signs suggested that the 600 ton tower could affect the structure of the church, and it was decided to dismantle it.